The Real Deal:

Social Media

Advertising

How To Be Successful In
Advertising On Social Platforms

Table of Contents

Introduction

Thank you for taking the time to download this book: *The Real Deal: Social Media Advertising*. I hope you find it to be helpful!

The first internet advertisement appeared as long ago as 1994. Viewers were invited to click their mouse to be taken to a website.

Things have come a long way. Since social media advertising began at the tail end of the nineties, it has grown to become one of the major marketing tools for all kinds of companies—start-ups, small, mid-sized, national, and international businesses all understand the importance of having a social media presence.

They also know that they have a captive audience on these sites for their brands.

At the completion of this book, you should have a better understanding of how to advertise on social media and how to do it well.

This book will evaluate the value of social media advertising as a whole. It will specifically look at five of the major options: Facebook, Google, YouTube, Instagram, and LinkedIn.

It will tell you the benefits each of these bring, and any potential pitfalls.

And it will take you through a simple step-by-step guide to getting your own advertisements in place on the site or sites of your choice.

Read on to discover a simple and effective way to drive customer traffic to your business.

Chapter One:
Why Advertise With Social Media?

The average American spends around six hours every day engaged in online activity. That time includes researching, working, and streaming films and videos, but over a quarter of that time is spent on social media—close to two hours every day. That is some audience!

Social media marketing is both a new and an established phenomenon. It is a very recent development for businesses, but the internet changes so rapidly that social media marketing is already old news. It is basically expected of brands to utilize social media now that the pioneering brands have already worked out the kinks.

What Are The Advantages Of Using Social Media Advertising?

If you are just now getting into social media advertising, you have some advantages over those who came in earlier. The early issues have been sorted, and most platforms now are easy to use and not overly expensive. Now, we can look at the advantages in more detail.

Brand Awareness

With so many potential customers, social media advertising is about more than instant sales. Building your brand awareness can help in the future. We can use an example to illustrate this. Let's say that you run a mobile car repair business. You are only needed by a customer when their car fails, but because they have been exposed to your business by social media, you will already be in their mind when they do need you. The added advantage is that since most social media advertising utilizes click per view or click per impression costs, your brand gets exposure free of charge in many incidences.

Customer Loyalty

In an oldish, but nevertheless interesting study by Texas Tech University, findings indicated that customers engaged through social media are more likely to be brand loyal. The reason for this is not clear, perhaps to do with the convenience and consistency of social media advertising, but it is nevertheless the goal of businesses to achieve brand loyalty.

Opportunity

Because your advertisement will be seen by so many people, each viewing is an opportunity for a sale. The conversion rate is not always high, especially at the beginning of a campaign or when a business is new, but opportunity is a key to success.

The Chance To Target An Audience

As we will see later, social media advertising allows business owners to refine the audience for their advertisements to the users most likely to engage. This is done by incorporating the details and behaviors social media sites collect about their users into the advertisement's visibility.

To illustrate this in its most detailed form, we can look at how major supermarkets use social media for incredibly accurate targeting. By tracking mobile phone use, they can see not only what their customers are looking at, but also how long they spend looking at those things. They can then use this information to target their advertising on social media.

While such detail is only currently available for those companies with multi-millions in their advertising budgets, the trend is always for technological break-throughs to become more readily available and cheaper over time, so who knows how long it will be before such analytics are available to all?

Free and Effective Feedback

Buying into expensive data analysis software packages is something that is beyond the budget of many small businesses, but social media can offer brilliant feedback. Simply asking for feedback—some companies offer inducements, such as entry into a prize draw or a coupon—will help businesses to know how their customers feel.

Strategies can be adapted in response to such feedback, with both marketing campaigns and customer services developing as a result of knowing what customers think.

Better Results

While by no means does every click result in a sale, the evidence suggests that the conversion rate of social media advertising is better than for other forms of advertising—about twice as high. Perhaps that is because of the targeting. Perhaps because it is on a "social" site, the ad is viewed more personally, as less of an intrusion than other forms. It also gets noticed more often, and because it appears on or close to something the user is interested in, it is more likely to be viewed. If you compare to TV and billboard advertising, the TV adverts are used as a time for chatting, making a coffee, or taking a bathroom break, and unless in a very specific location and time, such as a festival, billboard advertising just becomes unnoticed wallpaper. However, if the video you are watching on your social media platform is briefly interrupted by an advertisement, you'll pay attention.

A Global Audience

There are very few places in the world where people do not have access to—and are not obsessed with—social media. Indeed, take out North Korea, some Pacific islands, and parts of the Amazon basin, and it is pretty much universal. Your audience is only as limited as you want it to be.

Enormous Analytical Potential

For those with the time and expertise, it is possible to really dig into social media analytics to closely define your audience, their behaviors, and interests. This enables effective targeting for niche businesses that don't need to reach a large audience. They can instead specifically target the types of customers most likely to be interested in and purchase their products.

It also enables location-centred marketing to be effective. There is no point advertising your gardening services statewide or nationally when, in practice, you can only work within a thirty-mile radius from home. Social media advertising allows you to target such a narrow audience.

Social Benefits

Social media sites are renowned for promoting social causes. Millennials, who are the main users of social media (although older generations are catching up), are well known for supporting these causes. Anti-racism campaigns, humanitarian causes—there is a long list of causes supported by social media outlets. These can offer two advantages to social media advertisers. Firstly, engaging with these causes on social media gives you a good reputation among users and develops a sense of camaraderie between you and them. Secondly, companies can target and present their campaigns in relation to these causes. For example, companies can promote their green actions or their own social responsibilities.

Downsides

There are, though, caveats with social media marketing.

Firstly, it is important to stay up to date. Most users are younger people, and they expect content to be fresh and relevant. Leaving old information on your website or forgetting to update content for a few months can be bad for a company's reputation.

Next, not all platforms are right for all businesses. LinkedIn isn't really the right platform to advertise your new fast food place. Instagram isn't going to be a good tool for you unless you have lots of eye-catching images you can provide. Similarly, YouTube is best utilized with video content that you might not be able to produce.

Lastly, social media advertising is time-consuming. The people who use social media like to communicate. They like to message, share, and post. And they expect others to do the same. Social media advertisers can expect lots of questions, and they need to spend time addressing them or their reputation will suffer.

Nevertheless, the benefits in almost all cases outweigh the negatives.

We will now look at five major platforms for social media advertising: Facebook, Google, YouTube, Instagram, and LinkedIn. For each, we will consider the advantages and disadvantages of the platforms, as each has its own individual appeal. We will also look at how a business goes about setting up their ads in a practical way.

Chapter Summary

- Social media can reach a huge potential audience or be as targeted as you like.
- There are enormous advantages to advertising on social media.
- There are some downsides of which advertisers must be aware.

Chapter Two:
Facebook

Why Facebook? Well, size matters. When it comes to pure numbers Facebook is the main player; there's a reason it's the first name to come to mind when the words "social media" are mentioned.

As we noted in the last chapter, the average American spends an incredible six hours online every day, with over a quarter of that time spent viewing and engaging with social media. Forty minutes of that social media time (about a third of total social media engagement) is spent on Facebook. What do users do? They share and like posts: 4.1 million of them every minute.

More than this, it is estimated that over 1.5 billion people log onto Facebook every month, with the vast majority of those accessing via a mobile source. In August 2016, Facebook founder and creator Mark Zuckerberg announced that there had been over a billion visits to the site in just a single day.

The Facebook market is just too huge to ignore—and many businesses are already taking advantage of it. Facebook has around 50 million small business pages (interestingly, only a tiny percentage of these take advantage of advertising options).

In many parts of the world, including the US, UK, and Ireland, it offers small business advertisers live chat support, which is a fast and effective method of getting answers to questions businesses may have about advertising.

However, in recent times, Facebook has downgraded the visibility of its business pages, with less than half of one percent of followers seeing updates by the pages they follow. Although disappointing for business owners, it is one of the major ways that Facebook ensures its income, since businesses now need to advertise by buying ads.

On the plus side, the budget needed is not huge. A $100 investment has the potential to reach twenty thousand users. And, of course, one of the strongest advantages of social media advertising is that those people can be specifically targeted.

As long as the content on your website is good, business advertisers will also benefit from a wider audience, as advertisements, just like other posts, get shared by Facebook users.

Returning to the idea of targeting your advertisements toward certain groups of users, Facebook allows you to target your advertisements through a number of criteria. You can select:

- Age
- Demographics
- Gender
- Behaviour
- Location
- Interests

This is a powerful tool already, but even more than this, Facebook advertising allows businesses to be even more specific and:

- Customize an audience to build loyalty and nurture leads
- Create "lookalike" audiences that match your actual audience

- Make use of Facebook users' purchase behavior

Another weapon in the Facebook armory is remarketing. This is an option which shows ads for your business to browsers that have already visited your website, passed on their email address, or used your mobile app. It reminds people who have already demonstrated an interest in your business of what you can offer them and can double the conversion rate of views to purchases.

As we mentioned before, a high percentage of Facebook users access the platform via their mobile phones. Facebook allows you to add a "Call" option to your ads so that people can call your business directly from the ad. This can be a great tool because when somebody calls your business and actually speaks to someone, the contact is much stronger than a simple website connection. The call option makes person-to-person contact easier for customers to achieve—and these days, customers really want their purchases to be easy. If the customer can't get service quickly enough, they are likely to give up and take their business elsewhere.

The downside of advertising on Facebook is that, for some business users, the actual process of advertising is too complicated. Luckily, you have us here to help! We will break down the process of creating and placing your Facebook advertisements.

How To Use Facebook

As long as you can follow some straightforward steps, the process really isn't that complicated!

Making A Page

Step One – Launch Your Facebook Account

Many potential advertisers already have a Facebook account, and can skip this section. But for those who do not, here is the process for joining the social media giant: Signing up is really easy. Just visit the Facebook website, complete the short form, and click on the "sign up" button.

Note: It is a good idea to keep your personal account and business account separate. It makes privacy easier, and means you will not have to share passwords to your personal account. Plus, the way we want to be perceived professionally is often different from how we act in our private lives. That picture of you doing shots or dancing on a table might not be the best first impression for a future customer.

Step Two – Create Your Business Page

Create a page for your business and fill in all the relevant fields. This is not essential, but it is how most businesses operate and is best practice. This page is where you will promote the services you offer or the products that you sell. It is where you can interact with existing customers and reach out to new ones.

Step Three – Make It Visual

For businesses, the profile picture is really a branding tool. The logo or picture you upload will be the visual your customers associate with your business.

The next step is to upload a cover photograph. This is the first thing visitors to your page will see, as it covers almost the entire width of the top of the page. Therefore, be something interesting that represents your business. For example, if your business retails clothing, people dressed in your products would be a good image for this purpose.

Step Four – Content

Place a slogan or short description of your business in the appropriately named "Short Description" box. This will appear directly below your company logo, and it needs to sell your business straight away.

Enter the appropriate details to direct people to your website or create a new one specifically for your Facebook advertisements.

Step Five – Reach Your Customers

Now you are ready to begin launching your posts. Posts can be in the form of updates, videos or photographs. The most effective posts, according to Facebook itself, are those that are short (between 100 and 250 character posts generate 60% more likes than posts of other lengths). Visual posts are also effective, with many people preferring to process pictures rather than words.

What might you want to post? Well, returning to the clothing business example, you might wish to inform people of a winter sale.

Facebook offers a tool called Page Insights, which permits you to analyze your post's results so that you can refine your approach to targeting your customers.

Narrowing Down Your Audience

Once you are ready for business, the next stage is to target specific groups of potential customers and cater advertisements to them.

Step One – Creating Your Advertisement

On the right-hand sidebar of your Facebook home page is a section marked "Sponsored". Here you will find a button labelled "Create an Ad"—click on this.

Step Two – Make An Ad That Works

This section is extremely interactive, with previews popping up at every stage of the process. When you include photos, make sure that they are copyright free and available for general use.

Choose whether the ad will lead customers to a website or a Facebook page. There are several options here, but again, the process is logical to follow.

Step Three – Decide What You Want To Achieve

Obviously, we are after more sales, but it is the process that will achieve these that you now need to decide upon.

- Get more likes—likes do not equal sales, but they will increase the number of people who are likely to see your posts. So, for example, that post about the winter sale your business is having will reach more people.
- Promote a page post—this will increase the chances of a post you have made reaching its audience.
- Get new users—this will enable the targeting of people who are likely to use your app.
- Increase attendance—get people to attend a function you are hosting.

Step Four – Achieving the Right Audience

A blind, scattered approach to advertising is much less effective than a targeted approach. There are numerous options within the Facebook advertising program, including ones as detailed as targeting people on their birthdays and the filtering users by level of education. Time spent carefully considering these options will really help your business reach the right audience with its advertisements.

Once you have filled in the criteria, Facebook will give you an idea of the number of users your ad will reach. Even if the group is small, because it is a tailored collection, your success rate is likely to be good. Nevertheless, it is possible to expand the group without losing too much focus. You could consider other descriptors of your target group to increase the numbers Facebook identifies.

Step Five – The Size Of Your Budget

There are two ways to pay—you can choose to pay per click (CPC) or by impression (CPM). The latter often works out to be costlier, but that doesn't mean it is less cost-effective. You can set the currency by which you will pay, a daily or total budget, and the timings for your advertisements to appear.

Step Six – Check

There is an option to review your ad. You should do this. If, for example, you are advertising copywriting services and have made a spelling mistake, then your campaign is dead in the water before it starts.

Step Seven – You're Off

Place your advertising order. Credit card or PayPal can be used to pay.

Re-Focusing Your Campaign

Step One – Keep An Eye On Your Budget

It can quickly get out of control, so set your daily or total limit with care.

Step Two – Narrow Your Target

This might seem counter-intuitive. After all, if your campaign is not delivering the correct results then it seems obvious to increase your audience. In fact, Facebook research suggests that narrowing your target audience works better.

Step Three – Change the Visuals

Facebook shows ads based on how often they are clicked. They call this Click Through Rate or CTR. If your ads suddenly disappear, then that is because the CTR is too low. Although targeting delivers the most effective results, visual imagery is second. Swapping the picture in your ad might get more clicks. Therefore, it is worth keeping the pictures fresh in your advertisements.

Step Four – Think How Your Ad Will Be Viewed

Most likely, users will view your ad on a mobile device. Therefore, your ads need to be edited with this in mind. Facebook has a tool called Power Editor; which allows for editing ads to be most effective on mobile devices.

The process to get Power Editor is as follows:

- Only Chrome works for this, so open a Chrome browser.
- Go to the "Ads Manager" Facebook page.
- Click on "Power Editor"—it will appear on the left-hand side of the page.
- Install, download, and follow the instructions

Consider your ad placement in Power Editor. You can choose both desktop and mobile, or just one of the two. It is worth experimenting to see which offers the best results.

Step Five – Freebies

By creating an "Offer", you can increase your customers. People love something for nothing and this can stimulate loyalty to your brand. Set up a page where people can download a free code in return for their email address and name. You increase your customer base, and they get their freebie. Win, win.

Step Six – Focus On Your Customers

There is no doubt that people who already like your posts, your goods, or your website content are more likely to be repeat customers. Once your following is established, you can target these people, which means a better return on clicks. Since more are clicks are converted to sales, you can spend less money on your advertising campaign while getting better results.

Further Information

There are different kinds of ads that pop up in and around your newsfeed on Facebook. Here are a few of them that are commonly accessible with the Facebook Ads Manager:

Link Ads - These are the big ads that are most likely to pop up in the middle of a newsfeed. They allow for a large image and some space for content like a description and/or a URL link to a connected website or video.

Rail Ads - The perks of these ads are that they are inexpensive, and can be useful for retargeting a previously engaged audience on Facebook. They enhance brand recall among consumers.

Carousel Ads - These happen to be the most preferred ads these days, probably because people are used to swiping through things. The carousel style has become a convenient and quick way to introduce people to a multi-product brand or service. A carousel allows up to five products or services to sift through and select.

Lead Ads - These are simple ads that are displayed to generate leads. Generating leads involves gathering information from potential clients without being intrusive. A great example of lead ads would be the ones by blogs like Elephant Journal and Brainpickings.

Canvas Ads - The most recent introduction to Facebook ads are the canvas ads. They are a combination of link ads and carousel ads, meaning customers get to see these ads in their newsfeed while allowing them to sift through a bunch of products, videos, catalogs, and more offered by advertisers. Another benefit of canvas ads is that they are designed for a phone-based user interface but still cost almost the same as any other newsfeed ad. Canvas ads can be customized and made with the help of the self-serve tools provided by Facebook.

You should now be clear on the advantages of advertising on Facebook, and the method of actually getting your ads on this platform.

Chapter Summary

- Take advantage of the enormous number of potential customers Facebook offers.
- Spend time targeting your ideal audience.
- Keep an eye on costs and effects of your ads; re-focus when necessary.

In the next chapter, we will consider a second online advertising site—the giant that is Google.

Chapter Three:
Google

To advertise on Google, the simple-to-operate AdWords platform is used. We will look at how you employ this service to get your business known in the second half of the chapter, but we will start by evaluating whether advertising on Google provides enough value for the money.

There are both good things and bad things about advertising with Google. The main reason behind this is the size of the search engine giant. There are very few businesses whose name have turned into a verb, Hoover is perhaps one (for example, hoovering the carpet) and Google is even bigger. Logging on 'to google' some information is a phrase used millions of times every day.

So, on the one hand, Google can reach people beyond almost any other source, but that very size means that advertisements can be annoying, and get lost.

However, let's start with the positives.

It Targets People Who Are Already Looking for What You Sell

There is no other form of advertising where you have your specific audience at your fingertips. Certainly, TV works broadly in the area, for example, daytime TV features ads aimed at the elderly and unemployed – you tend not to see stair-lift advertisements placed during peak time early evening viewing. But properly targeted advertising on Google means that your ad reaches the people looking to buy your goods. When a potential customer types in "best hammer for sale in Chicago", your close by hardware shop is what they will see—in theory, at least.

No Lower Limits Helps Budget

There is no minimum purchase when you advertise on Google. This is especially helpful for small businesses, where the advertising budget can be tight. Start with a mere $20 outlay, and you can test the waters, review the results, and adapt your campaign accordingly.

Quality Feedback

Google AdWords offers the ability to track impressions, costs and clicks for all of your advertisements. It even offers the ability to add the phone and face to face visits generated by your advertisements to the online responses, to give a really clear picture of how your program is working.

Stay Ahead of the Competition

Research suggests that nine out of ten people use Google when they are searching for a service or a product. Once those searches go in, your competitors' names will come up. Just staying in the competition is a reason for using Google.

Free Advertising

Yes, and this applies in fact to any social media site which uses a Pay Per Click system. So, your advertisement only costs money if the user clicks on it. Therefore, even though you might not be the right choice for the customer on this occasion, they will still see your name and advertisement.

Quick and Easy

As soon as your AdWords account is up and running, advertisements begin to appear. This means that there is no delay in your name getting out there. The system allows for instant edits as well. Again, these are not unique selling points, but simply benefits that the platform offers. The platform also allows for instant cancellation. So, if your campaign is not working, then you do not need to offer a cancellation period.

Specific Targeting

In the same way as some other media sites, Google AdWords allows the user to specify an audience. So, for example, your hardware store in Chicago won't appear, unless you want it to, when the New York apartment owner is looking for tools to hang her pictures.

Additional Sites

Because Google is so large, your advertisements have the potential to reach an astonishingly wide audience, and not just through the main Google platform. YouTube and Gmail can both be used for your advertisements.

Despite these many benefits, Google AdWords is not for all. There are some issues with the system that business owners need to weigh before deciding whether it is the right destination for their precious cash.

Pay Per Expensive Click

The pay per click has its advantages, as we saw above, but for Google, those clicks can be extremely expensive. To get toward the top of the page, your business might need to invest up to $60 per click – and of course, those clicks do not guarantee a sale.

So, while that might be okay for companies with multi-million-dollar advertising budgets, it is not ideal for the small business.

Cheaper options are available, of course, but might not get you a priority position.

It Is the Home of the Big Boys

The principle behind AdWords is that key terms are used to induce your advertisement on the screen., but those terms are already in the hands of the major players, which means that start-up businesses can only get their foot in the door by paying extensively to use those keywords.

Character Limitations

We don't mean the uncertain reputation of your sales lead here, but AdWords has a very small limit on the characters you can place in your advertisement. This is not the end of the world, clearly, but does mean that planning the content of your ad is more difficult than with other sites.

Mistakes Are Expensive

Google will continue to charge for ads until your turn them off. So, for example, if you have taken down your landing page to make some alterations, but have forgotten to turn off your ads, you will still be paying for every click even though they take your customers nowhere (incidentally, meaning that they are almost certainly no longer your customers).

Google will inform you if there is a problem, but it often takes a while, perhaps costing your business hundreds or even thousands of dollars.

It Doesn't Fit Every Niche

Google works on a best fit basis, so if you are, for example, a car service that does everything from cleaning the car to touching up paintwork, when somebody searches for "Car Cleaning" you won't appear (at least, not before page 78 if you are lucky!) That is because your keywords also include the paintwork you offer.

Google AdWords, therefore, is not right for everybody, but if you decide that your business could benefit, this is how you place your advertisements.

The website Entrepreneur is one of a few that, while liking AdWords, feels it is not right for all. This article is worth a read, even though it is nearly three years old at the time of writing. It still provides food for thought.

Advertising on Google

At the time of writing, Google was incentivizing customers to place their ads with free ad credits. Making use of this can help you to see, in an inexpensive way, whether their campaign is on target.

Part One – Set Up

Step One – Starting Off

Go to the Google AdWords page.

For those with a Google ID password already, then that can be used as a login for AdWords. However, for those who do not have this, then they should select the "I do not use these other service'" option and create a new Google account with, for example a Gmail email address.

Step Two – Create A Campaign

By pressing the "Create Your First Campaign" button, you will be taken to the page to get your advertising set up.

Enter your webpage, with a specific target page if you wish. Then, begin to narrow down your target audience.

There are three sections to this.

- Location – this allows you to narrow down to country (usually the default option) or city.
- Network – Google will select the default option which runs ads on all its websites, although you can choose to narrow this if you wish.
- Keywords – these are words and phrases that you predict people will enter when they are searching for products.

Step Three – Set Your Daily Budget

Again, setting the amount here is a bit of a trial and error process. The figure needs to be large enough to allow you to measure results, but not so big that you end up losing your entire advertising budget in the first month.

It is probably best, though, to start conservatively.

You won't actually know straight away what your cost per click will be. That depends on a complicated auction process, which is why "masculine fragrance" is going to cost much more than "New bands from Belize".

Next you need to set your bids. It is best here to follow Google's default setting, at least until you are used to the system, although you can choose to set the price per click that you pay.

Step Four – Write Your Text

Remember, you don't have many characters to play with, so go for something catchy. Bear in mind, though, that Google is quite strict about its content. It will not permit false promises, so, "Free Ferrari" won't get approval, and it does not like over-hyperbolic punctuation or capitals.

But for all this, you need to catch your viewers' attention, tell them about your business and finish with a call to action, such as "Call Us".

Make sure that you use appropriate key words in the advertisement, as these are what searchers will have entered into the main search engine.

When you are happy, click on "Save and Continue".

Step Five – How to Pay

Click on the relevant payment method, that is usually by credit card. Before you hit "Save and Continue", make sure that you have included billing information. You will then be taken to a Review page, so check carefully that your details are correct. Then, advertisements will start to appear.

Part Two – Reviewing Your Campaign

Step One – Decide What Determines Success

There are many options here, and you should decide which one most closely fits your idea of a successful advertisement. Sales is one of the options available at this review point.

Some of these criteria are quite tricky to determine, and you may need to hire in an expert to do this work for you. It is probably best to keep your criteria simple, and have a go yourself, knowing that you might ultimately need some help.

From your criteria, you should be able to determine you Cost Per Action, or CPA. This is simply the cost each sale (or success criteria you have determined) incurs. So, if your Chicago Hammer needed an average of twenty clicks per sale, at twenty cents per click, then you CPA is $4 (20 clicks time 20 cents per click).

As the entrepreneur, you need then to make the judgment as to whether that represents value for money. Do remember, however, that each first-time customer probably costs more than repeat business. Once your client was happy with his hammer, he won't need to look on Google for his wallpaper paste, he will head straight for your hardware shop.

The final stage in the process is simply for you to decide where to take your campaign next.

AdSense

Although this service does not quite fit the purpose of this book, it is worth mentioning. This is Google's way of allowing website holders to generate income by hosting other companies' advertisements on their site.

Chapter Summary

- Google offers an almost limitless audience.
- It is not the best choice for every business.

Now on to the Google subsidiary, YouTube.

Chapter Four:
YouTube

YouTube was founded in 2005 and bought by Google the next year. It's the fifth most popular website on the internet at the time of this writing. YouTube is a free distribution site where people can upload videos of a wide range of content, from reviews to comedy to art and a lot more.

Why Advertise On YouTube?

One way of advertising on YouTube is to create your own video. This can be an effective tool, as well as great fun. There is a misconception that you must make a video which is funny, but this is only one genre that can generate interest.

You Can Reach A Global Audience

YouTube is the market leader in online video; therefore, your own advertising video can reach a huge audience, anywhere in the world.

Improve Your Ranking On The Google Search Engine

Getting on the front page of a google search is every business owner's dream. The links on your own video should inspire people to visit your website, to find out more about you and your product, thereby improving your business's ranking.

It Can Be Free

If your advertisement is a video you have made, it costs nothing to upload it.

You Could Create Your Own Customer Base

If you produce some good quality videos, then users could subscribe to your channel. Not only have you then got a collection of names and addresses, but also you know that they are fans of your products.

In-Video Adverts

The other way to use YouTube for your advertising needs is through getting them into other videos. This is a charged activity, but you benefit from attaching your advertisement to popular videos, where an audience is stronger than with your own video, and from linking the style of your own services or products with the topic of the video on which you have advertised. This is done via your AdWords account on Google.

Only Pay for What Is Viewed

There are two ways to pay for this form of advertising. First, you can pay by cost-per-view. We all know that 'Skip Ad' sign that comes up on most video; it is only when the viewer goes past this point that the charge is made. Second, you can pay per click.

Generally, the costs are a little lower than with straightforward AdWords, and it is still the case that a daily budget is set.

More Than One Way To Advertise

There are several ways of advertising on YouTube.

- In-stream – these are adverts which play before or during another video. You only get charged if a certain amount of the video is watched, but customers can leave the advertisement after five seconds. A side benefit of this kind of advertising is that it is getting your company name out there, because viewers are forced to screen the first five seconds.
- In-slate – these are charged when viewers watch the video, and appear in longer videos.

- In-search – these are advertising videos that come up at the top and side of the page when a user types into the YouTube search box.
- In-display – these are ads, again only charged on watches, that appear when other users have embedded YouTube videos on their own platforms.

You Can Still Target Your Audience

As with other forms of social media advertising, it is possible (and advisable) to target your audience. Filters include age, gender and demographic. It is possible to target by both topic (i.e. subject matter) and interest (i.e. general interests of the user, not specifically the video they are watching at that time). Key words can also be used, as can managed placements. These are specific pages you feel will work for your product. It is possible to advertise for all kinds of devices – mobile, desktop, laptop and so on.

How To Get Your Advertisement On You Tube

Here are the steps to follow. Before starting, you will need to have prepared your video and checked that it meets the technical criteria for inclusion on YouTube.

Step One - Go To AdWords

Set up an AdWords account as described in the previous chapter. Then, click on "All Video Campaigns" followed by "+New video campaign". Then, simply follow the instructions for uploading your video ready for display on YouTube.

Step Two – It Is Just The Same

Just as you would with AdWords (see previous chapter on Google for details), you will then set such matters as your target audience and budget.

Step Three - Review

Just as with AdWords, Google offers analytics to allow you to assess the success or otherwise of your campaign. You can then use this information to decide on the next steps for your advertising.

Because videos are an effective advertising technique, YouTube is a great site for developing a marketing plan. The downside for many is the actual creation of their video advert, or straightforward video if that is the route they have chosen.

What is important to remember is that the quality does not have to be amazing. Clearly, a small business is not going to achieve the production values of the latest Hollywood blockbuster's trailer. But it really seems as though, to viewers, that doesn't matter.

Chapter Summary

- YouTube offers the opportunity for free advertisement.
- It is excellent for creating brand awareness.
- Videos you upload do not have to be Oscar winners.

In the next chapter, we will consider Instagram.

Chapter Five:
Instagram

Even though advertising on Instagram is a relatively new phenomenon, especially outside of the United States, by March, 2017, over a million businesses were taking advantage of the social media site to promote their products.

One of the most important attractions of Instagram is the visual nature of its concept, with photos and videos being its content. A second major element is its immediacy; in some of its functions, uploads last just twenty-four hours.

Why Advertise On Instagram?

Visual Impact

With both photographs and videos able to be uploaded to the platform, Instagram is the perfect site for gaining a visual impact for your business. Most would agree that, because visuals are its speciality, Instagram is the most effective way of sharing this form of advertising.

The visual nature of the site also allows businesses to more readily spread their brand, making their products and services more identifiable when customers come across them in other settings.

Build Trust

Nobody really wants to read that much about your business's background, but through photos and videos, a lot of important information can be shared quickly and, more importantly, easily. That is, easily for the advertiser, and, also for the customer. The presentation of a short video or series of photographs can easily tell your story, thus gaining trust and support from customers.

Recognition

Creative ads have a stronger probability of becoming popular, even going viral, than ones with heavier written content. The information from the image is absorbed by the viewer with less effort than one that has a higher text content, making it more likely to be shared or recommended. These same factors mean that Instagram is also an ideal way to advertise promotions.

Ideal for Businesses Of All Sizes

There are ways, which we will look at later, of really keeping the costs down when advertising through Instagram, and this makes it an ideal platform on which small, as well as medium-sized and large businesses, can advertise.

How Do You Advertise On Instagram?

It is possible to advertise via other platforms, such as through a Facebook business manager account, but here we are looking at the simplest way to get your campaign going on the Instagram platform.

Part One – Getting Started

Step One – Open A Business Account

This is relatively straightforward. Use your phone to visit the Instagram website, enter your email and create a password. You will need to make it clear that you are opening a business account, and not a personal one.

You will need to create a username, so it should reflect your business. If you are a burger joint, "BarrysBurgers" would work. You may have to adapt slightly if your first-choice name has already been taken.

Step Two – The Objective Of Your Advertisements

As we have seen with other social media advertising opportunities, the platform will seek to help you deliver your key objective. With Instagram, there are a number from which to choose.

These include:

- Getting visitors to your website—this means selecting "Clicks to Website".
- You may want more than this, in which case, select "Website Conversions".
- "Video Views" is another option
- There are also alternatives such as an objective to promote engagement. The list is self-explanatory.

Step Three – Target Your Audience

The next step is as stated above. Filters exist to allow you to select age, language, behaviors and such. Location is another important filter. So, Boston-based Barry's Burgers will want to filter out Seattle living pensioners. By this point in the book, you will be familiar with how to target your audience.

Step Four - Budgeting

This section of the process enables you to decide the frequency of your advertisement, the timing of it and how much to spend. It is possible to choose between a daily budget and a total, or lifetime, amount.

It is also a feature that an advertisement can be run for a set period, so if Barry is doing a special hot chili burger for the month of May only, his ad can run just for the period of the promotion.

Advertising can be linked to Facebook AdManager, and costs are not enormous. A couple of dollars a day could reach up to a thousand users. If these are properly targeted, the returns should be worthwhile.

Step Five – Optimization Settings

Instagram gives you three choices here. You can select the default "Link Clicks". This uses clicks to your website to target an audience who already hold an interest in what you do. Alternatively, you can select "Impressions" which will offer a scatter-gun approach, hitting as wide a range of users as is possible within your limits, and there is a third option to send just one advertisement a day to users. This helps to avoid overkill, which can promote negative feelings among users.

Part Two – Methods Of Advertising

Photo Ads

This is still the most popular way of advertising. Simply use pictures of your product, your company logo and a bit of text to direct people to your website. You can target specific audiences with this, making use of the information they have posted. For example, Barry's Burgers is located close to one of Boston's beaches, so he could target people who have posted that they are looking forward to their day trip to the city for some sea air.

Video Advertising

The videos are short, perhaps an advantage over YouTube advertising, and those lasting less than half a minute work best. However, ads of up to 60 seconds are possible on the platform. Instagram developers themselves say that video watching is the biggest growth part of their business.

Instagram Stories

This is one of the more recent features in social media advertising. A full-screen video will tell the story of your business, or anything connected with it. Barry could tell his story of being head cook at the Ritz Hotel in London, England, but having a passion for both burgers and Boston driving him to serve the people of the city. A couple of happy eaters could tell of the wonder of his creations.

Carousel Ads

These are a series of ads that the user can scroll through. Barry can show pictures of his full range of burgers, each on a separate photograph rather than all cramped together on one.

Part Three – Making The Most Out Of Instagram

This part shows some of the tricks of the trade for getting the most from your business advertisements on this platform.

Your Bio Needs To Link To Your Website

At the time of writing, Instagram does not provide the ability to allow a click in the actual ad to get to your website, so you need to direct people to your company's bio to ensure that they can get to your website easily.

Use A Call To Action Button

Your business account section includes a "Call to Action" button option; Barry's "Call to Action" button might be "Get Directions", which could link to Google Maps or a similar app.

Chapter Summary

- Instagram offers a variety of ways in which to advertise.
- The visual quality of its platform means that it is a natural home for advertisements.
- There are size limitations for video uploads.

In the final chapter looking at specific platforms, we will focus on the business-orientated site, LinkedIn.

Chapter Six:
LinkedIn

LinkedIn is a business-oriented social networking site founded in May 2003. It has over 500 million registered users, from more than 200 countries. The profiles on LinkedIn work like personal resumes/CVs, except that they are available for everyone to look at and review. Like Facebook, you can connect with people on LinkedIn, but the types of people you connect with on Facebook versus LinkedIn are very different. LinkedIn is strictly business; you can connect with former and current colleagues, experts in your field, and prospective clients.

The good thing about LinkedIn is that its target market is well-defined. The site caters to business people, entrepreneurs, and professionals. If that is the market you are seeking, then your target is already set.

Why Use LinkedIn To Advertise Your Business?

You Know Your Audience

As we have outlined above, you know the people you are reaching. Further, because LinkedIn users include a resume in their profile, you can further dig down to a detail not available on other social media sites, where the best fit is usually just an impression created by their activities.

These impressions can be misleading. You might end up advertising to a mother whose activities were determined by her teenaged daughter using her account. That is not the case with LinkedIn, because you really know the people you are reaching.

Perfect For B2B Advertising

Business-to-business advertising is ideal for LinkedIn. This is because of a natural trust. Being a part of LinkedIn is a little like being in a club. While your business customer will still follow the usual due diligence before trading with you, almost certainly, you have the advantage that you, too, are a member of this social media club. Although it is a club, it is still a big one. Half a billion professionals and entrepreneurs use the site.

Effective Targeting

LinkedIn members are the right people to target with your advertisements. Eighty percent of members drive business decisions in their company or office, and they have twice the buying power of the average internet user.It is possible to maximize the effectiveness of advertising by targeting any of website targeting, contact targeting via email or account targeting.

A Professional Site

LinkedIn is robust in determining criteria for membership, and it is very professionally operated. In many ways, this makes it a safer medium to use for your advertisements. There is less chance of, for example, hacking or fraud.

Downsides

LinkedIn is very good, but it does have some elements that must be considered.

First, it is not the cheapest way of advertising. While this might be countered by the relationship between advertisements and returns, for the small business, on a tight budget, it might not represent the best value for money.

Second, to use it effectively requires a lot of time and energy. The basic set up (which we will run through below) is straightforward enough, but one of the ways the site retains its robustness is through the depth of its resources, which must be navigated.

Third, it is possible to feel it is a good move – with such a captive audience – to put all your eggs into one basket, especially when it is a high-quality but expensive basket. Although it may have 500 million members, that does not mean either that: a) they are all active; or b) everybody you wish to target is a member. There is a risk of missing out on some of your potential market.

Part One – Joining LinkedIn

Step One – Set Up Your Basic Information

As with other platforms, opening an account is the first step. The quickest way of doing this is by using your Facebook account, but if you prefer not to do this, the process for direct joining is self-explanatory.

Next, you will need to set up your profile. Remembering the nature of other users, who, if your advertising is successful, will be visiting your profile, it is important to make this section impressive.

The profile will be returned to later in the set-up process. That is the point at which you add things like your educational background. Uploading your photograph occurs at this point. Pick a professional- looking one! You should also add specialities to your profile, such as specific skills you can offer.

Step Two – Build Your Connections

Here is where you establish the contacts you already know, or wish to get to know. LinkedIn provides an optional service to scan your email account to speed up the process.

Step Three – Make Yourself Public

You will want to add as many contact points as possible, to best promote yourself and your business. Your website address, blog details and other social media account information is sensible. However, do be careful with the last of these. Personal stuff could damage your reputation – what we get up to at the weekend or on holiday is stuff we may not wish to share with potential customers!

Step Four – Build Your Base

LinkedIn will now offer possible connections based on your profile information. Since you wish to build your contact base as large as possible, then take this opportunity.

Part Two – Improving Your Presence

Step One – Get Recommendations

Since prospective customers will see these recommendations, it is a good idea to go out and seek them. Try to be specific in these—a general "It's amazing" recommendation doesn't tell people very much, so try to target connections (your contact base) who can talk about specifics related to you or your business. For example, ex-colleagues are a good option.

Step Two – Build Up Your Connections Through Introductions

This is done by asking your existing connections to introduce you to their connections. This can be done by browsing the connections of one of your connections.

Another way of building your connections is by joining an appropriate LinkedIn group.

Step Three – Keep Up To Date

Regularly update your profile. This brings two benefits. First, it demonstrates that you are active and on the ball, crucial characteristics for high-powered customers. Second, when you update, those on your LinkedIn network will be informed, reminding them of your presence.

Step Four – Stay In Touch

On such a large site, it is important to invest the time to stay in touch. Sending a note of congratulations when a member connected to you gets a new job, for example, can help to keep you at the forefront of all your contacts' minds. It is also, of course, a nice thing to do!

Part Three – Get Advertising

You could skip straight to this stage, but with a site such as LinkedIn, it is the trust that is built up in you that generates sales. So, spending the time getting yourself represented and recommended is a great way of maximizing the quality of responses to your advertisements.

Step One – Create An Account For Advertising

You should now sign in to the advertising section of LinkedIn, "Campaign Manager".

Step Two – Choose Your Ad Style

There are three advertisement forms with LinkedIn. These are outlined below:

- Sponsored Content – using this form of advertising allows you to get updates to more people, target the appropriate audience, and set your own budget. There are some analytics available also to measure the effectiveness of your campaign.
- Text Ads – these are simply created ads which can be targeted to your audience. You can pay per click or per impression, and only get charged for those that get results.

- Sponsored InMail – this form allows you to personalize your advertisements, and can be effective in driving users to, for example, webinars or conferences.

Once you have decided on and created your ad, there is the facility to review it before it goes live.

Step Four – Build Your Audience

Using feedback tools, you can modify and increase your target audience to expand the market you can reach.

As a final point, we will just briefly touch on blog writing. LinkedIn is a different platform for advertising than other sites. It has a kind of exclusivity that, for example, Facebook just does not possess. This means that your customers are buying into you as much as they are buying into your products. One way of establishing your reputation, growing a following, and promoting your products and services is through blogging. LinkedIn offers its own blogging site. It is easy to use (simply click on the "Share an Update" button) and get writing. Images and videos can be included, and it is even possible to share your blog beyond LinkedIn, if you wish.

Chapter Summary

- Advertisers gain access to those with the most spending power.
- Membership of the site helps to breed trust.
- It is perfect for B2B advertising.
- Users need to spend time keeping their profiles and connections up to date.

Chapter Seven:
Some Success Stories

For our final chapter, we will look at some success stories. We are going to concentrate on small businesses, and see how their use of social media advertising has helped their company to flourish.

Picture Perfect

JarvieDigital Photography is a photographic site specializing in wedding and nature photography. Clearly, being a specialist photography agency has its advantages—the pictures tend to be pretty good. However, the company has used its skills in two specific ways, which have generated enormous business for their site.

First, they differentiate their campaigns through two different platforms – Google and Facebook. On Google+, he focuses on sharing his expertise and resources; this helps others and expands his fan base. On Facebook, the services the company offers are promoted.

The lessons that can be learned from studying JarvieDigital's approach are:

- Be prepared to provide advice and giveaways to develop enthusiasm for your business.
- Target different platforms for different purposes.

Blissful Advertising

An ice cream company called Coconut Bliss, was one of the pioneers in seeing the advantages of social media advertising. They took advantage of what was, in their early days, a new way of advertising, by using superb photographs of their products in action. They also used social media platforms to generate interest in their special events. Today, the company has generated over 30 thousand likes on its Facebook page, and is going strong.

The lessons that are still applicable are:

- Use top quality photographs.
- Use social media advertising to promote special events.

Tea Time

David's Tea, a specialist company in the field of beverages, took the approach of using social media to get their story and profile across. Using as many techniques on as many sites as they could—including Twitter, which we have not specifically analyzed in this book—they sought to make their name known.

A quick check shows that the company has 85,000 followers on Twitter, and even has its own Wikipedia page. That is excellent coverage, and a major reason for the success of the company today.

The lesson here is simply to put energy into your social media campaign. Don't go into it half-heartedly.

Final Words

When it first appeared, social media was considered by many cynics as a passing trend that would be gone when the 'next big thing' came around the corner. Those people will have eaten their words.

Social media is probably the biggest innovation on the planet in the last ten years. It is, without doubt, here to stay.

We hope that from reading this book you have gained the following information. You have seen the general benefits (and potential disadvantages) of using social media to promote your business through advertising.

You have seen that this advertising does not just have to be in paid advertisements; through blogging, and setting up a page, you can attract interest.

You can then build this interest through specific, paid marketing. Of the many and growing numbers of social media platforms, you have seen in some details the advantages of using Facebook, LinkedIn, Instagram, Google, and YouTube.

Another advantage, indeed almost a requirement of social media advertising, is the feedback element. The best businesses listen to feedback from their customers, and adapt in the light of these comments. Small businesses which cannot afford to buy into complex and expensive data analysis software systems, successfully look at the feedback their customers offer through their social media posts to develop their own business strategies.

And finally, you have seen a small number of examples where the use of social media advertising has led to great success for a business.

Your own company could be the next one to create sales for your goods and services through advertising on social media.

Thank you for reading this book!

Made in the USA
Columbia, SC
29 November 2017